AF580038

This book is dedicated
to
Madhuri and Seamus.

Written by
Sushima Shekar

Illustrated by
Santhya Shenbagam R.

Vikram and Aadhi are excited to go on a trip to India.
Aadhi and Vikram say bye to their dad who had come to the airport to give them a send off.

This is a **special** visit!

They will get to see the Navarathri festival for the first time.

Vikram talks non-stop during the trip about what he will do when he arrives in India.

He was thinking of his last trip to India when he went to the **zoo, beach, park and malls.**

But this time, says Amma, he'll get to see Paati's special golu display.

What's golu?

Amma explains that Navarathri is celebrated by setting out a doll display called **Golu** for 9 days.

At the end of the 9 days - which is what "Nava Rathri" means - a puja is done to get blessings from the

Goddess of wealth - Lakshmi,

Goddess of power - Parvathi and

Goddess of knowledge- Saraswathi

Vikram and Aadhi are very excited to see the dolls!

Thatha, Paati, Mama and Mami are at the airport to receive them. They go home together happily.

As Aadhi and Vikram enter the house, their eyes widen in wonder.

They have not seen anything like this before!

In the living room, all the furniture had been removed. In its place, a beautiful display of various **Hindu Gods** are adorned on nine steps.

It's the first day of Navarathri!

"Look, Christmas lights" cries Vikram, while Aadhi runs to take all the dolls that are within his reach.

"Aadhi," says Vikram. "You cannot touch them. You can only see them." But Aadhi doesn't care. He's trying to stack one doll over another.

Paati says, “Now both of you must eat and sleep. Tomorrow morning, we will tell you the stories about each doll. And in the evening, when visitors come, you can tell them the stories yourself!”

They reluctantly go to bed, giving orders that the Christmas lights should not be switched off.

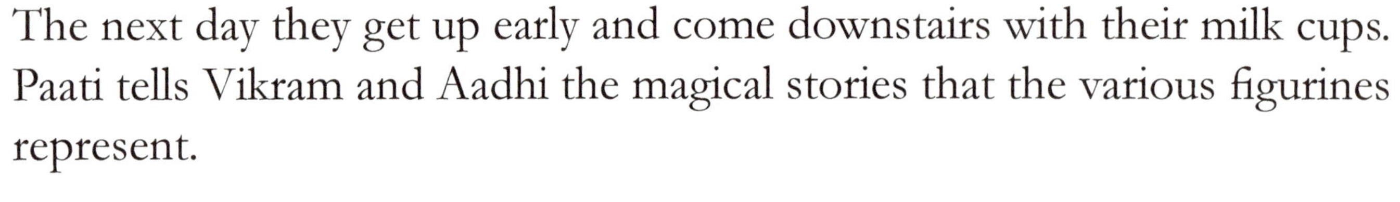

The next day they get up early and come downstairs with their milk cups. Paati tells Vikram and Aadhi the magical stories that the various figurines represent.

The stories of Krishna Leela, Adi Sankara making a poor woman's roof rain with golden gooseberries, the temple car procession, the story of Gajendra Moksham, and more.

Vikram and Aadhi are both fascinated by the Ganesha Cricket set, the various vegetable sellers and marketplace display, and most interestingly, a hill made from actual wet mud with a temple on top and small sprouts of coriander acting as trees.

Mama and Mami sit with them on the floor and patiently explain the meaning behind each display, while showing them how to handle the dolls carefully and put them back.

In the evening, visitors come to see the Golu and meet Vikram and Aadhi. The boys are dressed in finery, and give the guests Thamboolam bags when they leave.

"Goody bags!" insists Vikram.

Whenever guests ask them about the various dolls, Vikram eagerly tells them the stories he's learned, while Aadhi sweetly hands over the dolls themselves.

They have a fun time for all nine days. Paati, Mama and Mami take them to see the golu displays at friends and relatives' homes as well.

But each time, Vikram comes back and says, **"Our house Golu is the best."**

The ninth day is Saraswathi Puja.

Paati asks Vikram and Aadhi for their favourite books to stack in front of Goddess Saraswathi, along with the books from the rest of the family. Paati applies Chandan and Kumkum to all the books. She lights the lamp and keeps the Prasadh (delicious offerings of food) before the Gods, and asks them to repeat this Sloka:

"Saraswathi Namasthubyam Varadhe kaama roopinim
Vidhyarambam Karishyami sidhir bhavatu me sadha."

They sweetly repeat after her.

Then she does an Aarathi with the lamp, and distributes the prasadh to the children, family and friends.

Now it's time for them to go back. Their father has been missing them. They miss him too! They are ready for their flight back to America.

Paati and Thatha advise Aadhi and Vikram to be nice to Amma, to listen to her and to come back soon with Appa.

They say bye at the airport, each holding their favourite dolls from the Golu.

About Navarathri

The story of Navratri is the celebration of good defeating evil. The demon, Mahishasura, blessed with immortality by Lord Brahma, wreaked havoc. The only caveat to Lord Brahma's boon was that Mahishasura could be defeated by a woman. To stop his atrocities in the 3 worlds, Brahma, Vishnu, and Shiva – pooled their divine energies to create Goddess Durga, a symbol of supreme strength and power. Armed with 10 weapons (Trishul, Sudarshan Chakra, Sword, Vajra, Spear, Snake, Lotus, bow and arrow, mace and conch) and spirits as powerful as a lion, she battled against Mahishasura for 9 days. The demon tried several tricks to confuse and disorient the goddess. But they did not work. As soon as he took the form of a buffalo, Maa Durga's trident found its mark, ending his reign of terror.

Thrishakthi
Baalambigai
Tanjore doll
Goddess Mahalakshmi
Hayagreevar

Paavai

Goddess Meenakshi

Hanuman
Goddess Shakthi
Goddess Lakshmi
Goddess Saraswathi
Krishna
Balavrama

Machavatharam

Koormaavatharam

Kalki

Parasurama

Narasimha avathaaram

www.ingramcontent.com/pod-product-compliance
Lightning Source LLC
LaVergne TN
LVHW071129160826
845679LV00005B/1222
9798897244898